YOUR KNOWLEDGE HAS VALUE

- We will publish your bachelor's and master's thesis, essays and papers

- Your own eBook and book - sold worldwide in all relevant shops

- Earn money with each sale

Upload your text at www.GRIN.com
and publish for free

Bibliographic information published by the German National Library:

The German National Library lists this publication in the National Bibliography; detailed bibliographic data are available on the Internet at http://dnb.dnb.de .

This book is copyright material and must not be copied, reproduced, transferred, distributed, leased, licensed or publicly performed or used in any way except as specifically permitted in writing by the publishers, as allowed under the terms and conditions under which it was purchased or as strictly permitted by applicable copyright law. Any unauthorized distribution or use of this text may be a direct infringement of the author s and publisher s rights and those responsible may be liable in law accordingly.

Imprint:

Copyright © 2007 GRIN Verlag, Open Publishing GmbH
Print and binding: Books on Demand GmbH, Norderstedt Germany
ISBN: 9783668581920

This book at GRIN:

http://www.grin.com/en/e-book/380761/social-and-technological-factors-influencing-kenya-s-organizations

Teddy Kimathi

Social and Technological Factors Influencing Kenya's Organizations

GRIN Publishing

GRIN - Your knowledge has value

Since its foundation in 1998, GRIN has specialized in publishing academic texts by students, college teachers and other academics as e-book and printed book. The website www.grin.com is an ideal platform for presenting term papers, final papers, scientific essays, dissertations and specialist books.

Visit us on the internet:

http://www.grin.com/

http://www.facebook.com/grincom

http://www.twitter.com/grin_com

SOCIAL, CULTURAL AND TECHNOLOGICAL FACTORS WHICH ARE INFLUENCING KENYA'S ORGANIZATIONS

WRITTEN BY

TEDDY KIMATHI

PUPLISHED IN

2007

Table of Contents

Social and technological factors which are influencing Kenya's organizations 3
- (A) Social forces : 3
  1. Pollution 3
  2. Changing values 3
  3. Poverty 3
  4. Employment and education 4
  5. International financial institutions' emphasis on sustainable development 4
  6. Change in the people's lifestyle and living standards 4
- (B) Technological forces : 5
  1. Information and communication technologies in distance education 5
  2. Environmental concerns 5

Does culture influence our perceptions? 7

Whether human resource managers should consider one's personality as critical job performance factor 8
1. Morale 8
2. Learning ability 8
3. Experience 8
4. Culture 8
5. Attitude 9

REFERENCES 10

Social and technological factors which are influencing Kenya's organizations

(A) Social forces :

1. Pollution

During the last few years, Kenyan organizations have become conscious of a serious problem regarding their physical environment. Firms and industries cannot continue to produce goods and then carelessly discard waste without upsetting the balance of nature. Pollution affects the land we use, the water we drink and the air we breathe. The survival of mankind depends on how well the society controls its natural environment.

When Kenya was 'young', pollution did not show its great effect on the land, water and air. Few goods were produced and the population was small. Now that we have more than 30 million people and the quantity of goods produced is so great, that the environment is seriously affected.

To curb this problem of pollution, local governments and environmental agencies have passed control laws. Business firms have become more conscious of the needs to take deliberate – sometimes – costly actions to help improve the physical environment.

2. Changing values

Mankind's values are generally rather stable for long periods. There are times however, when values undergo change. Evidence suggests that during the past few decades in Kenya, values of Kenyans and Kenyan organizations have been shifting. The changes is brought about in part by such factors as pollution, poverty, consumer unrest, expanding population and corruption.

Society is concerned about the quality of goods and services provided by organizations and the quality of the environment. The desire to improve the human side of life has been especially evident among youth. Poverty, discrimination and corruption are some of the problems which firms and organizations have tried to fight until now.

3. Poverty

The poverty income level, which is not the same for all, is based on family size, age of members and location. For instance, in slum dwellings, most of the families are unable to save enough money for investment and future uncertainties because of many mouths to feed, children to educate, clothe and give health protection.

As a result of these factors, organizations have really concentrated on provision of job security, fair and better wages and salaries, supporting trade unions and also creating a band or partnership with micro financial institutions, in order to raise the living standards of workers, and in general maintaining customers and consumers, since they will be having more money to use in some interactions.

4. Employment and education

A large labor force is necessary to support a large GNP. As the population grows, the labor force also grows.

The labor force is composed of all those people who are available for work, whether they are employed or unemployed. Not included in the labor force are those people under 16 years of age, full – time students, housewives and retired and handicapped people.

With improved technology, the need has come for additional skilled employees. The demand for accountants, managers and other business specialists, for example, has never been greater. To become skilled, this means that the workers must be educated.

While demand for skilled workers has been rising, the need for unskilled workers has been declining. A problem to the businessman is to find adequately trained employees. Education and specialized training, therefore, must be readily available, in order to ensure that Kenyan's economy becomes industrialized.

5. International financial institutions' emphasis on sustainable development

The idea of "sustainable development" emerged from policy discussions at the United Nations throughout the 1980s and was popularized in the lead-up to the UN's high-profile environment and development summit in Rio de Janeiro in 1992.

Merging the language of long -term sustainability from the environmental movement with the "development" discourse of neo -colonialism, sustainable development became a rationale for advocating the continued expansion of capitalist market economies in the global south, while paying lip service to the needs of the environment and the poor.

6. Change in the people's lifestyle and living standards

The constraints presented by poverty and by related issues such as illiteracy and the impact of poor health and HIV/AIDS, on efforts to respond to the challenges of ageing are still being addressed by various scholars, intellects and economists in various organizations, whether governmental or not.

Stressing the impact the HIV/AIDS pandemic has on most African countries, particularly to those people living below the poverty line, has really reduced the costs that most organizations incur, since money that was being used to treat HIV/AIDS workers and employers, can now be channeled more in productive projects like investments, savings and innovations.

Mankind is ageing and the older population is growing. Policies in the area of ageing must be revised and adjusted, taking into account the new demographic and socio-economic factors of today. We must all be fully aware of the implications of the role of older persons in society, in particular in a world characterized by globalization and epidemics, such as HIV/AIDS. Being aware of the positive contributions that older persons can play in social development, the Kenyan government has established policies regarding health and the fight against poverty and illiteracy.

(B) Technological forces :

1. Information and communication technologies in distance education
Instructional technology, according to current definition of the Association for Educational Communications and Technology is "the theory and practice of design, development, utilization, management and education of processes and resources for learning (Seels & Ricky, 1994)"
Rajesh (2003) examined the problems associated with information and communication Technology (ICT) adaptability is developing countries in the context of distance education. He said that the communication technologies had come to play vibrant role in democratizing education not only in the developed, but also in developing countries. The problems associated with the growth of ICT that had been focused upon in his study were the political, economic, cultural and technological factors.

2. Environmental concerns
The deep reductions in emissions required for addressing climate change support the conclusion that technological change is needed. Although we know in which direction this

technological change should go (more energy – efficiency and low – carbon energy sources), it is not always acknowledged in the instructional design of international treaties, or even in domestic legislation, that technological change is more than the mere change of technologies.

Technologies are introduced at a certain pace, which is not only determined by economic factors such as incentives, but also, by user preferences, habits and turnover factors that are specific to the technology. Indeed, different social factors adapt technologies in different ways. Social factors can be as diverse companies, governments and individuals: consumers, end – users and citizens. The considerations for technological change can vary significantly across these factors.

Does culture influence our perceptions?

I think culture influences our perceptions, since the society at large is the one which influences what we accept or decline, in the form of dress code, language, character, education, beliefs and attitude or what we are generally comfortable with, as a community. First, the character and structure of an organization is affected by beliefs. Beliefs may include religion and superstitions. For religion, an organization's dress code, style of service, language and sale of products(s) may undergo a change which will work hand in hand with the needs of the immediate society or community. For instance, a bank mainly dealing with savings in the Egyptian countryside have to improve the way it convinces its customers to save and earn. Interests, since the locals in that area believe that earning interest is stealing, which is a sin to God.

Secondly, an organization may also be affected by the attitude of the people who are also its competitors, employees, customers and investors. Attitude is the positive or negative way of thinking, acting or feeling. As far as an organization's success of profitability is concerned, people both in the external and internal environment of a firm should have a positive attitude towards research, promotion and development, in order to ensure that the organization operates in an effective and efficient manner.

Thirdly, institution is another powerful tool which influences the way an organization functions and relates with the society at large. Churches, mosques, temples, synagogues and families have strongly contributed to the creation of present policies and laws which have made firms to be more organized and morally disciplined.

For instance, an organization that is dealing with marketing of products will have to avoid using pornographic images on its commercials, since that is not acceptable in all faiths. Explicit commercials can also disintegrate families, due to lost morals and traditional customs.

Values are other instruments which culture uses to mould the way an organization thinks, behaves and perceives things or situations in an appropriate way. Values refer to conduct and language, which has been shaped by teachers, elders and advisors over a long period of time. Therefore, values cannot be separated from a firm or an organization, since they are deeply ingrained in the people's minds. A good organization is the one which appreciates different values and formulate policies and rules to unify these values.

Whether human resource managers should consider one's personality as critical job performance factor

I think human resource managers should consider one's personality as a critical job performance factor. The following aspects should then be taken into consideration.

1. **Morale**

According to Flippo, morale is a mental condition or attitudes of individuals and groups which determine their willingness to co-operate. Good morale is evidenced by employee enthusiasm, voluntary conformance with regulation and orders and willingness to co-operate with others in accomplishment of the organization's objectives.

2. **Learning ability**

For an individual to be employed and to operate successfully in an organization, he or she should have curriculum vitae, and well conversant with the organizational philosophy and have familiarity with the shifts in technological factors and information.

Following rules, procedures and culture of a particular organization requires a person to be well equipped with skills, strategies and creative ideas, which will help him or her in contributing to the achievements of an organization's goals or adapting to its environment.

3. **Experience**

Any person, who wants to fit well in a particular organization, should be well oriented with all the activities and policies which his or her "dream" organization entails. To carry out a particular task, one must be well experienced with his or her area of operation. Such tasks may be in specializations like marketing, productions and operation, employees' supervision, and also accounting.

4. **Culture**

An organization can't work effectively and efficiently if an individual's belief and values are not taken into consideration. Wise managers and directors are the ones who balance the views of different cultures with the organization's objectives.

For instance, a worker who is a Buddhist cannot work well in an organization which deals with caging of stray dogs and cats, since Buddhism emphasizes on freedom of both humans and animals.

5. Attitude

This is a positive or negative feeling towards something. An individual's attitude is a very important instrument in creating good morale. An employee's motivation may be influenced by the internal and external environment of an organization. A worker's attitude may be determined by factors like: discrimination, level of pay, geographic conditions of the workplace, level of security, reward systems, leisure hours and also the nature of policies.

REFERENCES

Bernard A. Shilt, Kenneth E. Everard & John M. Jahns(1973). Business principles and Management; 6th Edition. South – Western Publishing Co., Ohio, USA.

John R. Schermerhorn, Jr. (1999). Management; 6th Edition. John Wiley & Sons Inc., New York, USA.

The World Bank (2000). Entering the 21st Century; World Development Report 1991/2000. Oxford University Press Inc. New York, USA.

Ingrid Waldron & Robert E. Ricklefs (1973). Environment and Population; Problems and Solutions. Holt, Rinehart & Winston Inc.,Philadelphia, USA.

YOUR KNOWLEDGE HAS VALUE

- We will publish your bachelor's and master's thesis, essays and papers

- Your own eBook and book - sold worldwide in all relevant shops

- Earn money with each sale

Upload your text at www.GRIN.com
and publish for free